The Wealth

of the

Highly Fabulous

Renewed Mind

Dr Patricia Benjamin

Publisher: HFW Publishing Ltd

Distributed by: HFW Publishing Ltd

ISBN: 9781092730723

Dedication

To everyone who has decided not to accept the hand they were given but who has realised wealth starts in the mind. To this person I say, "You can be wealthy, if you think you can".

CONTENTS

About the Author

Acknowledgements

Preface

Chapters

Frequently Asked Questions about Wealth

A Note from Dr Patricia

About the Author

Dr. Patricia is an award winning Media Personality; Leadership Coach and Mentor; Women's Empowerment Speaker; Songwriter and Producer; Publisher and Editor-in-Chief and ordained Pastor. She is deeply passionate about working with young girls and women to own their fabulousness and live the fullest expression of their lives in every way.

Having spent ten years in the local community providing pastoral ministry and care, particularly for women, Patricia saw the need to work with them not just spiritually but holistically.

She began to concentrate on some areas such as self-esteem, personal confidence, relationships, and life purpose. In doing this, she received a great response from so many women and went on to qualify as a professional Life Coach.

This opened a brand new path for her in professional development and transformation, and opportunities within the media presented themselves. Within months, she was sought out by Channel 4 Television to provide life coaching for women on a new series focused on mothers and daughters and shortly after Dr Patricia began an exciting career in radio. This led to her being recognised by the prestigious Sound Women 200 as a woman doing amazing things in radio, alongside other women such as Victoria Derbyshire, Angie Greaves, Moira Stuart, Vanessa Feltz, etc.

Patricia uses her total life experience which includes her background in the pastoral ministry, the commercial world, and the media industry to inform all she does.

She is a London representative for Christian Women in Media and the UK Chief Operating Officer for American cancer charity, Making it Matter. As well as winning the Black Entertainment Film and Fashion Awards for Best Radio Personality, Patricia is also listed in the Top 100 Most Influential Black People in Digital/Social Media.

In 2017, during International Women's Month, Patricia was inducted into the Women Appreciating Women Hall of Fame; a privilege she was delighted to accept.

In July 2017, she was also awarded a Leadership honorary doctorate degree with letters from United Nations University for Global Peace, which she considers a tremendous honour as a peace builder with a global vision.

Patricia and her husband Christopher live in London where together they have raised four children and thoroughly enjoy watching them create their own paths through life.

Acknowledgements

I want to thank my family for their support and all their efforts throughout the writing of this book. They have all been on this journey with me and we all have learned so much. I wish them all that is good is this world

Preface

Why the need for this book about money, wealth and success?

Well, I for one have read several books on the subject over the years but it is not until this moment that I have become ready to attain it. It is only now that I have found myself completely happy and at peace with the idea of being rich and wealthy.

Before now, money simply paid the bills and provided for other necessities and then anything else came after. I did not see money for what it truly is; an empowerment to live a fulfilled life; a means of attaining what you want and need in life. There came recognition that wealth was the empowerment to succeed on a larger scale, not just a means of driving a better car or living in a bigger house; it was far more than this. Money and wealth are exciting topics, not the sole domain of boring business men or idle pleasure seekers.

I have come to a stage in my life where wealth is now a comfortable normality. I have a new paradigm which allows me to actively pursue wealth and actively work towards increase.

I am now completely at home with running my business on a much higher level. Nothing has changed except me, my outlook and my way of thinking.

I now enjoy the money making process. It is not a hard thing to make money. Money is not hard to come by. Money and wealth are all around me. However in the past I was not tuned in. Consequently, money was hard to come by and it was hard to attain. Now things couldn't be more different for me. Yet, the world hasn't changed; all that has changed are my feelings around money, my feelings around wealth and how they apply to me. Now, wealth and my life go hand in hand. This is the Wealth of the Highly Fabulous Mind. It is a transformed mind. It is a mind that sees all things as possible. It is a mind that sees there are no limits except the ones I impose. It is a mind that has demolished arguments that rise up that would seek to contain and restrain. It is a mind that brings into captivity every negative thought that would contend otherwise. This Highly Fabulous Renewed Mind has set out its position and works from its intuition.

Wealth is not something I seek for, it is something I have. In every situation I always have more than enough for my wants and desires; my necessities; and to give away towards charitable donations.

This book is for those who are aspirational and may be struggling to get their businesses off the ground or who are otherwise seeking success in life. I want them to know that the abundant life is theirs by divine right. I want them to know that they were not put on earth to live a life of mere survival.

Now to the person who asks about the starving millions in Africa or even for that matter, in many first world countries? I say to that person, what about the millions who are doing well and succeeding? If you live in close proximity to someone who is doing well, it shows it can be done in your part of the world. It shows that person knows something that you do not know. You cannot blame your background as people from your background are succeeding. Rather than continue to stay as you are, take a leaf out of their book, learn something new, and change your life. It is up to you.

It is important to develop a mindset that has absolute clarity on self belief and does not have the attitude that someone will come and rescue you. You are your own rescue. You can save yourself. Would you rather sit and wait for the cavalry? Some white knight? What if they never come? How much better to take responsibility for your life, take note of your abilities and find a way to use them to profit and succeed? Others have done it and you can too. You can take back your power too. You can have a victor's mindset and not a victim mentality.

Let us look at someone such as Oprah Winfrey whose grandmother, the woman who raised her, was a maid. Oprah recalls the moment when her grandmother tells her to watch her work so she would know what to do when she grew up and took up similar work. Oprah says she knew deep down, instinctively, that this would not be her portion.

This book is written to the Highly Fabulous Woman who has come to the conclusion that she is worthy of wealth, of living an abundant life, of living a life of joy. This book will uncover the lies that kept that wealth locked away from her, the lies that kept her back from experiencing the abundance that life had to offer her and instead open her up to her fullest expression of the greatness within her.

Having wealth will empower her to serve others in a greater way. Having wealth will empower her to influence a great many more people than before possible. Having wealth will help her do everything to the standard she truly desires and deserves.

I am writing this book because I am so passionate about helping to facilitate a complete shift in thinking around money, wealth and success. I am sharing everything that has worked and is continuing to work for me and I want you to take it and run with it and go all the way.

It is time for the Wealth of the Highly Fabulous Renewed Mind to come into view.

Let's talk.

Dr Patricia Benjamin

Chapter 1 – Exploding the Lies Around Money

"I refuse to feel guilty. I feel guilty about too much in my life but not about money. I went through periods when I had nothing so somebody in my family has to get stinkin' wealthy" **Jim Carrey**

Coming from a very spiritual background, money was not something I ever sought after. I knew I needed money to pay for things but I had no ambition in particular to be rich. I look back now and believe that I subconsciously held the view that having what I needed was the most important. I did not aspire to wear designer brands, yes I would like them, but they were not things I was particularly interested in or drawn to.

I will use this chapter to look at some of the lies and limiting beliefs many people have around money, many of which I subconsciously held myself.

Lie No. 1 – God gives us only what we need, not what we want.

I remember being aware of the thought that God did not give us what we wanted but instead He gave us what we needed. This thinking did not lead one to think extravagantly but to think in line with only what was absolutely necessary, what was a priority, and what really mattered.

This is actually a very big lie. God does not just give you what you need. He actually takes pleasure in giving you what you want and what you desire.

The very bible instructs us "whatsoever you <u>desire,</u> when you pray believe you receive it, and you shall have it." Well, that certainly puts paid to that theory. These are the words of Jesus himself. He does not preface his words by saying this only applies to the bare necessities of life, instead he uses the term 'whatsoever you desire'. He also states that just as we human beings know how to do good things for our children, how much more our heavenly father would give good things to those that asked. I also read in the Psalms where the writer, King David, is thanking God that his desires and his needs were met, so that his youth was renewed. Is David saying that having your needs and desires catered to is actually anti-ageing? If so, I think he has a point because worry and stress over the struggle to provide for life's basic necessities is truly not good for the skin and causes those worry lines and wrinkles.

David is making the point that he did not just have his every day essentials but he had things that were for his own good pleasure.

Coming from a spiritual view point this was a significant discovery. I wondered then why many spiritual people had such a problem with wealth. In fact numerous people in the bible were super wealthy. They were not broke. Where do we get this idea that just having enough for your own needs is what is acceptable? If we serve an abundant God and Jesus himself states that he came to give us abundant life, how did we ever figure that wealth was not a good idea?

You do not have to poor to have humility. To have humility is not to walk around with less than everyone else and be content. To have humility is not to believe you must stay in your allotted place. To have humility is not to think you are less deserving than anyone else. To have humility is not to believe that you are not worthy of success or wealthy. Here is a definition of humility for you. Humility is agreeing with God as to who He says you are. It means accepting that His plans for you are good, to give you a future, to prosper you and to give you a bright expectation for your life. Humility is agreeing with God that you are His child and therefore a very precious individual; an individual with greatness inside you. Humility is agreeing that you have a rich spiritual heritage and you should live in such a manner.

So let's explode the lie that you cannot be spiritual and rich and wealthy. Let's explode the lie that God wants to keep you poor so you can be humble. Let's explode the lie that God only gives you what you need, i.e. your bare necessities. Let's nullify and cancel that right now.

And God is able to make all good things come to you in abundance so you may have all sufficiency in all things. 2 Cor. 9.8

I will bless you, make your name great and you will be a blessing. Gen 12.2

But you shall remember the Lord your God because it is He who gives you the power to get wealth. Deut 8.18a

It is good for one to eat and drink and to enjoy the good of all his labour,... for it is his portion. Every man to whom God has given riches and wealth... this is the gift of God. Ecclesiastes 5:18, 19

14

This is such a crazy one. Imagine saying that money isn't important. If it were not important why would countless millions go to jobs they do not like in order to get it? Why would people commit crime to get it? Why would we give money to charities? Why would we give money to churches? Money is important because everything costs. You can get nothing without money. You cannot make your house payment, you cannot keep the lights on, you cannot keep food on the table, you cannot help those in need, you cannot provide for schools and education, you cannot provide for health, you cannot do a lot of things without money. It also stands to reason that the more money you have the less you have to worry about providing the necessities of life, of helping those you love, or assisting in your community. Money helps provide peace of mind. It helps lessen stress. It helps keep your blood pressure down. It provides shelter and nourishment. It helps us buy the things that make us happy, such as entertainment, music, arts, drama, and the like. Money helps us support causes we believe in, provide medical care and attention for those who need it. How can we ever use the expression 'money isn't important'? Of course it is. The Proverbs say 'money answers all things'. It is better to be wealthy than impoverished. Being impoverished or poverty stricken is not a desired state for anyone. Never accept the statement that money is not important because without it you will not be able to live your life to its fullest expression.

How many people do you know that desire to do certain things, or begin projects but the critical point is they do not have the money? However, this is where they should become creative and resourceful, it is not the point where you sit back and give up. This is where your inner resources should come into play, but we will talk more about this later.

Money isn't the most important thing in life, but it's reasonably close to oxygen on the "gotta have it" scale. **Zig Ziglar**

Lie No. 3 - You have to work really hard for money.

So first, let me ask the question, how many people do you know that work really hard, from morning till night and they are only just over broke?

How many hard working, conscientious, good people work hard all their lives and are nowhere near rich or wealthy? Yet how many people have had an idea which they have worked on and committed to that has made them wealthy? To be wealthy you need to exercise strategy and wisdom. You do not need to work hard in the sense of working your fingers to the bone. The work that is required is the inner work.

Your outer world of attitudes, wealth, work, relationships and health will always be a reflection of your inner attitudes of the mind. **Brian Tracy**

People who are unable to motivate themselves must be content with mediocrity, no matter how impressive their other talents. **Andrew Carnegie**

I have concluded that wealth is a state of mind and that anyone can acquire a wealthy state of mind. **Edward Young**

Wealth is the product of man's ability to think. **Ayn Rand**

Lie No. 4 - Money Changes People

Well money doesn't really change people; it merely allows them the freedom to express themselves more fully and more freely. So a person who was selfish will still continue to be selfish but it will be more noticeable. Before they were wealthy you could say, "well they can't afford to help out". Now you will see, they can help but they choose not to. They were always that way. Money is not the root cause of anything.

Money gives you the freedom to do with your time what you want to do with it. **Richard Branson**

Lie No. 5 - Money is the Root Cause of Evil

I wish when people would quote the scripture they would quote it fully and in its full context. The actual scripture says the Love of money is the cause of evil. We are not supposed to love money for its own sake. Also the intent behind that verse is the miserly attitude behind money, that is, those who are miserly and unwilling to give and so keep and hold onto their money; that is the kind of love for money that is being talked about. That same chapter talks about God giving us all things richly for us to enjoy. In this book we are going to acknowledge the role that money plays.

When the scripture is quoted it must be put into context. For example we all know the story of Solomon who asked God for wisdom. God was so pleased with his request that God gave Solomon riches and untold wealth as well as wisdom. Now please understand God will not give you a blessing with something that is evil. There are many people in the bible that God blessed with wealth, so He is clearly not against it. What we must not do is love it to our own detriment.

Lie No. 6 - Money Corrupts

There are some who believe that those who are rich somehow got it by oppressing those who are poor, or by immoral business practices or by other dishonest means. It must be said that there are all types of people, both rich and poor. You have people who are poor who are quite capable of oppressing those even worse off than they are and you have others who are rich who are kind and generous. All people who are rich did not come about it by cheating someone else. Many did so by launching successful businesses, others by inheritances. There are those who win by games of chance and luck; however these rarely last long term as those who win in this way have no paradigm to sustain their wins. They are not acquainted with wealth and end up bringing themselves right back down to the level they are familiar with.

Lie No 7 - Money Makes you Self-Centred

18

This is another amusing one. You do not have to be rich to be self-centred. There are people who think about themselves and put themselves first all the time who are not rich. That is who they are. You have people with no money who are always thinking of ways to make more. You have those who are always coming up with some Get Rich Quick scheme. Then you have those with plenty of money who are always thinking of ways to hold on to it, and ensure they don't lose it. You have those worried about their stocks and shares. It is all a question of how you choose to think. Money does not in itself make you self-centred or selfish.

Lie No.8 – It is Good to Give without Expecting Anything in Return

This is a principle that goes against everything in nature. Nothing just happens. For every action there is a reaction. If you sow a seed in the earth there will be a resultant harvest. If you give money to charity you expect that money will go where it will do good. If you keep giving away and keep getting nothing in return, then you will be the one in need. This makes no sense. It is appropriate to make a profit, to receive a harvest and to see increase. That is how this entire world works. People provide value and they are compensated. Everything works on expansion and increase. It does not work on reduction and decrease

Lie No.9 – You cannot be Rich and Spiritual

This is such a big lie. I would like someone to please tell me what is so spiritual about being in poverty. What is so spiritual about not being able to pay your bills? What is so spiritual about owing people money? What is so spiritual about being in debt? The bible says to owe nobody anything except to love them. How can being broke, being in debt, not being able to feed your children or send them to a good school possibly be spiritual?

Do we see God as being broke? Do we see God as being in poverty? If God, who we all would accept as being very spiritual, is not broke or in debt, then why do you need to be?

In fact we are told that God is the source. We are told that everything belongs to Him because He created it all and He gave us everything freely to enjoy. He tells us that "the gold is mine and the silver is mine".

It is truly time to debunk this very unspiritual theory that being rich and being spiritual are diametrically opposed because they are not at all. Let's move on, nothing to see here.

Action Step 1

1. Look at each of the money lies in the chapter and make your own list of money lies that you may have subconsciously been holding on to.

2. Ask yourself how believing and accepting these lies have influenced you so far in terms of setting financial goals or life goals.

3. Ask yourself what living your life in alignment with these money lies has cost you.

4. Take each money lie, one by one, turn it to its polar opposite and create a new belief around it. Once you have formed the new belief, embed it by acting on it.

5. Begin approaching your life with these new beliefs and ways of thinking.

6. Create a journal where you explore this new way of thinking, and develop your consciousness around it.

PERSONAL NOTES

PERSONAL NOTES

Chapter 2 – What is Your Money Script?

"I was raised to have value for money, to have respect for money, even if you have a lot of it." **Jennifer Lawrence**

So we all have a money script. That is, a narrative in our heads when it comes to money.

This script most often starts from childhood and by the things we heard around money. You would have imbibed these subconsciously. Now this script could actually be quite positive and work well for you. It could be a script that tells you that making money is easy. It could tell you that you should always negotiate for your worth. It could tell you that money is a sign of success; that the more you have the more you do; that money should not be wasted but used wisely and not frivolously. It could tell you its right to buy the best that you can afford. Or it is say that money just causes problems; that people only love you for your money, or that it is best to spend as little as possible and to hoard as much as you can to give security. It could even tell you that it's best to be safe and keep most of your money for a rainy day. Your script can do you a service or a disservice.

Let's examine whether your money script is serving you. Let's examine where you got it from. Let's decide if you want to upgrade it.

Give me the boy and I'll show you the man. **Jean Piaget**

This is what absolutely excites me. We can decide to upgrade our script. You can upgrade to a later model. You can sign up to a new

24

way of thinking. If you take a look at your life so far and are pretty happy with yourself financially it may be that you have always had a healthy approach to money. If however you sense you are underperforming when it comes to negotiating a business deal, or when it comes to choosing something of high value, just for the sheer pleasure and enjoyment, without any guilt attached, you are probably due an upgrade.

One way to do this is to adopt new beliefs. You can adopt a new view. You can choose to take a new position.

I did this very quickly by changing the type of people I would listen to. I chose to listen to people who were successful and who considered it normal. I chose to listen to those who were achieving good results in business and were happy to share the methods and process. I chose to listen to those who saw wealth as a means to an end. I chose to listen to those who saw wealth as desirable because it gave them freedom. I chose to accept that it wasn't the luck of the draw who became wealthy. I chose to accept that I could make new choices that would impact my income. I chose to take new action to change my position.

Once I made that choice it was interesting how new opportunities began to seek me out. It was fascinating to notice that I was attracting that which I was seeking. It seemed the more I learned and understood about wealth, success and money, the more I entered into that realm. It seemed the more I focused on levelling up, the more I became in line with my new vision.

It seemed as though when my thinking changed then my view changed. It seemed as though when my view changed my reality changed.

Could I really just think and grow rich? Was it really that simple?

The answer is yes and no. Yes, you must think rich to grow rich, yet that rich thinking must lead to taking inspired intelligent action which will bring about the desired results.

So the important thing about changing your paradigm, meaning changing the way you see the world, is to change your source of influence. I chose to aggressively change the information coming my way. If the information so far had not lead me to become wealthy, then listening to more of the same would not do so either.

If you want to know the future, look at the past. **Albert Einstein**

I realised that until I changed or reprogrammed my mind, my past would be a great indicator to my future; this meant I definitely needed to renew my mind by transformational thinking. As someone who loves to read, I sought out books that would explain in detail the process to wealth, the process to success in business, and I would devour them. Once I had absorbed the teaching I would endeavour to put them into practice.

The first time was scary but once I had crossed that bridge, it was game on.

Next I had to see myself as someone who could feel comfortable earning high levels of income and as someone who had value to give that merited such.

Once I saw the life changing and transforming value of what I did, I was able to recognise this should be reflecting in my fees. I also recognised that I did not have to try to please everyone. I realised I needed to focus on those who saw the value of what I gave them and who were not intent on taking as much from me as possible and giving as little as they could get away with in return.

When this began to happen I started receiving high calibre clients. These were clients who understood this method of exchange and would accept no less themselves. So what happened was that I began working at higher levels in society. When I recognised my value, society recognised my value.

When you choose to recognise your value then those around you will too, and those who wish to interact with you will automatically come correct.

This is a way of changing your paradigm.

Another way is to consider the people you spend time with, it's important that they are similar thinkers. If this is not the case it can be easy to just fall back into old ways of thinking. It is time to level up in terms of your circle. Do not try to bring the old circle with you; it's more likely they will exert more pressure for you to remain. What is more effective is to demonstrate by doing. Once they see the change in you, if they like it, they will ask questions and you can help them then.

Action Step 2

1. *Choose 3 books you can begin reading daily that will help you upgrade your money script.*

2. *When you read these books ensure you make notes in your journal on the lessons you are learning and what you have taken away from each book.*

3. *Decide to do something different based on what you are reading. If you just read without taking action it will not help you. Choose an action you can take from each book and implement it quickly. Speed to implementation is key. Get your momentum up and running*

    Book suggestions

    Think and Grow Rich by Zig Ziglar

    You Were Born Rich by Bob Proctor

    Feeling is the Secret by Neville Goddard

PERSONAL NOTES

PERSONAL NOTES

Chapter 3 – The Truth about Money

Success doesn't come to you...you go to it. **Marva Collins**

The truth about money is that it's necessary to have plenty of it to live a life to its fullest. That is to say, to be able to fulfil your purpose at its highest level. It is impossible to succeed at high levels with low level money. In order to function at a high level, high level money is required. This is where you either to decide to demand of life your portion or you decide to settle. You perhaps look at your peers and think you may as well just fit in and do something similar, or you look at your parents and grandparents and decide they made do and were happy and that perhaps you should do the same.

Wealth can be a choice. It is your choice.

You can decide, whatever your starting position, that wealth is a clear goal for you and that you will work towards it.

Once you have come to that decision it is imperative that you stand behind it. It must be a quality decision which means you do not back down or retreat from it.

An important element to this is to be very clear as to why wealth is desirable and necessary for you. A strong 'why' must be the driver and motivator behind your decision. This is necessary because wealth will not just come. Wealth has to be courted. Wealth has to be pursued. Life will test you to see if you are serious. Circumstances will appear to mock you as you lay your claim. This is the reason why your deep desire and determination to be wealthy for a purpose must be in place.

It is not enough just be tired of the status quo. Many people are tired of the status quo but they are still not moved to do anything different. It is as if they have given in. It is as if they have lost their nerve. It is as if they no longer really believe it can happen for them.

Your 'why' must be more than just a want. There are many people who want things but are not prepared to do the work. Wealth requires work. It requires mental and emotional work, not just physical toil.

Many people say if you work hard you will be rich. However you are and I both know there are generations of people who have toiled hard from sun up to sun down and have never been wealthy. This shows us that physical toil is not the root.

Wealth will begin in the mind. Once you are wealthy in your mind, the rest will catch up.

The scriptures tell us that we should prosper even as our soul (mind, will and intellect) prospers. This means that as we grow and develop our understanding and consciousness we are able to create prosperity.

I wish that you prosper and be in health, even as your soul prospers. 3 John 2.1

We cannot create what we cannot understand. One way to grow and develop a wealth consciousness is to listen to those who are already wealthy.

You do not need to know these people personally. You can access them through their books, their seminars, their talks etc.

There are those who are wealthy who will give you general advice but no real guidance. I have heard those types of people say to just trust God and begin your business and God will bless it. I am sorry. This is not enough for you to step out on faith.

Faith does its homework. If you want to begin a business you can look at those who have successfully run a similar business to the one you desire and see how they went about it. Learn the lessons. Success will leave clues. You do not need to reinvent the wheel.

Then there are those who are successful that will give you practical and honest guidance on how to get started and how to go about things.

Let these people be your mentors.

Becoming wealthy can be done scientifically. That is to say by following a set method and process which will bring a set result. If it has been done before it can be repeated.

This does not mean you will not make mistakes or situations will not go sideways, however a good foundation will be the difference between ultimate failure and ultimate success.

The most important thing is the story you are telling yourself. This story must revolve around the fact that no matter what happens wealth is your goal and until then you will not stop.

Empowering yourself financially is very necessary as it will put you in a position of influence and financial independence. This is something desirable and it is something that can be yours when you have financial freedom.

Actions Step 3

1. Ask yourself why you want to be wealthy. Sit down and consider in depth the true reason you desire wealth.

2. Once you have come up with this answer please write it down in your journal.

3. The reason for this is to discover the true motive and reason which is what will keep you on track as the journey to wealth is rarely linear. Remembering why you want wealth is key.

4. It is important too because you can assess how real your desire is. This is because your desire for wealth must ultimately be connected to your purpose and your destiny. Everything works together when you step into purpose. Once you see where wealth fits into your destiny you are more likely to pursue and succeed. We make this distinction because this book is to enable you to live beyond just being able to meet your every day needs and wants etc. It is all about enabling you to have an impact on the world and wealth enables you to do so in a great fashion. If you do not have wealth, you will be limited. This book will give you keys to live a life of freedom in every way.

PERSONAL NOTES

PERSONAL NOTES

Chapter 4 – A New Money Paradigm that Works

Your world is only as small as you make it. **Gabrielle Union**

Your money paradigm is always working. Until now it has been working subconsciously and producing the fruit you are currently enjoying.

Now we are focusing on adopting a money paradigm that is working for you in a positive way.

From now on you want to adopt an attitude that wealth and riches belong to you now and not that it is merely coming. You want to adopt a paradigm where good opportunities naturally come to you; a paradigm where you get high calibre clients easily; a paradigm that accepts significant sums of money come to you regularly from multiple sources; a paradigm where you are contributing financially to causes that matter to you; a paradigm where you are able to make a difference to someone who is in need; a paradigm that enables you to give easily to charities and good works; a paradigm where you are able to sponsor someone's education that is not in a position to pay for it themselves; a paradigm where you see yourself totally free to do whatever you desire. That is financial freedom.

This is not fanciful. People actually live like that. You can too. First of all you have to see it as possible for you. You have to see it as accessible to you. You have to see it as a viable goal.

Once you do so you can begin.

Recognise the repeated negativity of thinking and speaking and expecting has brought you here. Now you are changing that by the same process. In other words, you will consciously change your thinking, your speaking and your expectations.

One of the most powerful ways of reprogramming your thinking is the use of affirmations.

Affirmations are positive statements that you make consistently with emotion and feeling. You do not just say words lightly. You say them with intensity. You say them from the heart, not by mere routine. This is called 'doing the work'. This is your new job for the present.

You are in the process of rewiring your brain so it thinks differently in a certain area.

You want to think differently in the area of finances and in particular, wealth. So create 10 new positive statements about money and repeat them daily for at least 21 days.

We choose 21 days because that is how long it takes to create a new neural pathway in the brain. This is why it takes 21 days to create a habit.

Begin thinking now what those affirmation statements might be.

Your affirmation statements must all be in the affirmative. I know that seems obvious but I have seen affirmation where people say what they are not or what they do not want. For example, 'I am not poor'. This is not an affirmation. The correct affirmation here would be 'I am wealthy' or 'I am rich' or 'I am abundant financially". I hope this helps you as you create your affirmations. You must always say what you want, instead of what you do not want. Focus.

Action Step 4

This is one of my most favourite exercises and I hope you will love it too.

> *Go out in your mind one whole year ahead. Then look back over the past twelve months. As you look back you will see that you have just had the most successful and most wealthy year of your life.*
>
> *What has happened in that year? What have you achieved? What did you do to accomplish the success you now have? Create in your mind's eye that entire years' trajectory.*
>
> *Think about changes you experienced emotionally, spiritually, mentally, financially and physically. How did it all happen? What did you start doing differently? How did things begin to turn around? What kind of person did you become?*
>
> *How does it feel? How do you look? How do you feel about yourself? How do people respond and engage with you? Take your time during this experiential exercise. You should embrace it fully and go at it full on. Do not be half-hearted. Go all the way.*
>
> *Take as long as you like.*

I love to play instrumental music whenever I do this exercise; it makes it so much more tangible for me and easier to do.

When you have finished open your journal and make notes on what you did during that wonderful year you just envisioned and make a plan to begin doing just those very things in real life.

This is a great way to get a vision for your life. It's your vision. It's your life. We are told without a vision the people perish. Do not perish. Get a vision for your life. It's your choice.

PERSONAL NOTES

PERSONAL NOTES

Chapter 5 – The Renewal of the Mind for Personal Wealth

We read in the bible that we are to be transformed by the renewal of our mind.

We cannot be transformed by simply adopting a new image. We can adopt a new look, a new hairstyle and yet if we haven't changed the way we feel inside it has no true or lasting meaning.

There are so many people who have gone through plastic surgery because they feel if only they could just look different they would feel different and feel better about themselves. To some degree that is true. However when it comes to long standing and deep-seated issues, the task is more than that. The change needs to take place in their mind. The transformation comes through renewing the mind.

This is what this entire book is about. It is to encourage you to change your money story, to change your money script, to change your money paradigm and that entire process is really about renewing your mind.

When we replace old thinking with new thinking a great source to go to is sacred text. These words are already infused with life and spirit and absorbing these and declaring them can only accelerate the process.

If you return to the Almighty, you shall be built up...you will lay up gold like dust... the Almighty shall be your defence and you will have plenty of silver. Job 22. 23-25

Now let's talk for a moment about mindsets generally. Isn't it interesting that the New Testament talks about prospering and being in health, even as your soul (your soul comprises your mind, will, intellect, imagination, conscience, intellect and emotions) prospers.

Your thoughts around money are so powerful that we must pay special attention. Thoughts are things. They exist on a spiritual level. They exist on the quantum field. Your dominant thoughts around your money must be positive because your thoughts will draw to you their very essence and their physical component.

A sacred principle you can adopt is that of 'calling those things that be not as though they were'. This is simply saying what you want as though it is a present reality. So you speak as though it is already the case. You are not asking for it, you are accepting that it is yours and you speak as though you are already in possession of it. You not only speak as though you are in possession of it but you act as though you are already in possession of it. You speak it with feeling. Feeling it is so important. You act as though it's happening right now.

This is exciting.

I learned recently that the late music icon Prince used to practise being a superstar before he was even known by the public. He would do things like go to the gas station to buy gas and refuse to go out of the car to pay for it because he was a star and his public would mob him, so his friend had to go and pay instead! This was when he was completely unknown. This is a perfect example of living now how you want it to be.

This may seem strange but it is a powerful spiritual principle and a powerful psychological principle.

You can renew your mind by acting out what you are saying. You can renew your mind by acting out the things you are reading and learning. You can renew your mind by quickly implementing your fresh new thoughts and ideas as they come. Do not sit on your learning. Act on them.

You also renew your mind by saying thank you.

The sacred text tells us if we ask for what we desire and we believe that we receive them, then they will be ours. So what is the appropriate behaviour and response when you have been given something you asked for? Of course you know the answer, you say thank you. You show appreciation. You show gratitude.

Being in a positive, appreciative state of mind is more appealing and in line with wealth than constant worry and anxiety about not having enough. Instead renew your mind with joy, peace, thanksgiving, appreciation of what is lovely and good and full of virtue.

This is a rich and wealthy state of mind.

This state of mind is in alignment with your Creator who every day loads you down with benefits.

As you practise being grateful and consequently create an environment around you that is conducive to what you desire, allow yourself to feel what you are speaking. Remember words are energy. Allow them to crystallise in your mind and flood your heart, and feel them inside you. Declaring your thoughts is very powerful. Just hearing them said out loud activates your faith and hope within you. It is empowering and it's a God given ability. It is a divine ability to be able to imagine, to say and then create. I love the spiritual principle of calling things that are not as though they were. It translates and transfers the idea from the unseen to the seen, from the quantum realm (accessed through your God given image centre - imagination) into the Now. Science tells us that not all mass (substance) is visible. Faith is the invisible mass (substance) from which we create. It is the substance of the renewed mind.

"Faith is the substance of things hoped for, the evidence of things not seen". - St Paul

Action Step 5

1. *For this you need to go into your personal laboratory. This laboratory is in your mind. It is called the Imagination. Your Image Centre. Begin to see yourself as wealthy and enjoying financial freedom.*

2. *Imagine how you look. See yourself wealthy. What does that look like for you?*

3. *Imagine a typical day. Begin from the moment you wake up until you go to bed. What does your wealthy life look like?*

4. *Describe what you love and enjoy the most about your day.*

5. *Enter into this experience fully. Literally sit down where you will not be disturbed and imagine a day in your new life. See it. Believe it. Have it.*

6. *Finally give thanks. Be grateful for all you have received. Be appreciative for your blessings. Be happy and joyous about your life in that moment. Feel everything as though it's happening now and be thankful.*

PERSONAL NOTES

PERSONAL NOTES

Chapter 6 – The Frequency and Vibration of Wealth

It is not until you come to a spiritual understanding of who you are that you can begin to take control. **Oprah Winfrey**

I am so excited that we no longer see science and God as in conflict. As we discover the laws upon which this universe works it is more and more apparent that science is confirming and revealing God and His creation. One of these laws is The Law of Vibration and Frequency. This law is even greater than the Law of Attraction that people talk about. This Law of Vibration is the basic and primary law. It says that everything is moving and that nothing is stagnant. Everything is in constant motion. If you remain the same you are not living. If you are not moving you are dying. The Law of Vibration is the primary law of life. This is because we are all energy. We are all spirit.

We all have personal frequency and sometimes that changes daily. We don't use the word frequency when talking about our person; we just say 'how are you feeling?' That is an everyday expression to ascertain the frequency of that person. When you are vibrating on a certain frequency it can be felt. When you are in a good place both emotionally and spiritually it can be felt. You cannot see emotions or see spirituality but you can feel them, or sense them. This is your frequency.

Well, the entire universe operates on frequencies and wealth has its frequency; what we must do is operate on the frequency of wealth. Have you noticed that poverty carries a certain frequency, or feeling?

It is a feeling of struggle and desperation that does not even have to be uttered. It can be felt. It is a feeling of lack, inadequacy and quiet desperation which needs no words but is very real. At the same time wealth and riches also have frequency. It is one of freedom. It is one of peace. Peace is a powerful component because it means that you are not troubled. It means you are not anxious. It means you are not burdened down. You are free and light. That is the feeling and frequency of wealth.

This is the frequency and vibration you want to become accustomed to. This will become your new vibration.

So to get on the same frequency and vibration as wealth you must assimilate thoughts and feelings in line with wealth.

It is time to put away feelings of inadequacy, feelings of lack, feelings of 'life is a struggle', feelings of being born under an unlucky star, feelings of being one of life's losers. Change your feelings to that of loving life. Change your feelings to strong expectations of good things happening for you. Change your feelings to expectation of receiving good news. Change your feelings to everything working out in your favour and for your good. Change your feelings to being first in line for blessings. Change your feelings to being ready for good success.

The sacred text tells us that God's blessings make us rich without adding sorrow.

Get into feeling peaceful, serene, at ease and appreciative of your next breath.

Feel grateful and happy for your loved ones. Feel grateful and happy that you are in your right mind and you are alive right now. Feel thankful for all the opportunities for success all around you.

These are the vibrations that will get you on the frequency of wealth. This is where you can now tune into the frequency of that which you desire.

Do you see how differently you are approaching money now? Do you see how much your views and thoughts towards money have changed already? This is all part of the renewal process.

Now it must be said that sometimes we do not feel great, we do not feel in a high vibration, we do not feel peaceful.

It's at these times we must learn to take control of our state and learn to change our state. I have several ways of changing my state and I am going to share them with you. Use ones which work for you and create a few of your own.

Music

Music is a powerful God given gift and the right music can change how you feel and change your environment almost immediately. Find music that is uplifting with positive words and harmonious sounds. When I need to raise my energy I choose upbeat songs that get me moving and get singing along. Creating motion with my body changes my emotions too. I shake off any feelings of heaviness or boredom or frustration and lose it all in the music.

Sometimes I use music when I pray or when I meditate. I will choose beautiful sounds that wash over my spirit and bless my heart and uplift my emotions.

Nature

Nature is also a powerful way to reconnect with my own peace and often going for a walk in a local park filled with trees, streams, birds, flowers and plants is just a gentle way of calming the mind and bringing relaxation. It reminds me that the world is working in perfect order and everything is as it should be and all I need to do is get in the flow.

My Words

Because I know that every word carries a vibration, I check and see what I have been saying, even to myself. If I find my words are out of alignment I give myself a pep talk and talk myself up and out of any mental mess I am facing. It works every time.

Prayer

I take prayer so seriously because through it I am able to enter a dimension or state beyond myself. We are spirit beings and when through prayer we connect with our Creator, we are strengthened in a powerful way. Using your spiritual prayer language is especially wonderful to build yourself up. (*Jude 1.20*)

Beauty

Enjoying beautiful things; arts, poetry, silks and fabrics, paintings, and all creativity. Immerse yourself in beautiful things. God has given us a beautiful world to enjoy. There is so much beauty to embrace.

Recreation

This is a big one. Sometimes I can get so focused on my goals that I forget to relax and have fun and do things just for the sheer enjoyment. We need recreation time too. This for me can be calling up my girlfriends and doing a girls lunch, going to a comedy club together, or it can be going to see a girls flick at the cinema, going to get a makeover at the makeup counter or it can just be an afternoon out window shopping followed by cupcakes and cocktails.

Remembering the Times

Sometimes I look back at some of the things that have happened in recent times and take courage from them. It's easy to forget what you have already accomplished when things are not working out well in the present and confidence is in danger of being lost. Remembering times of previous success can be encouraging.

Favourite Exercise

Sometimes a good physical challenge is just the thing. So a gym workout or a brisk walk or a hill climb hits the spot.

Helping Hands

It's also good to see if there is something I can do to help someone else. It's good to get the focus off yourself at times and spend time doing something for someone else without expecting anything in return. This is a random act of kindness and it always feels good.

Up the Ante

Sometimes what I need is to challenge myself. I find that sometimes I am in a low vibration because I am bored. This means I need a new focus or a new challenge. So, I begin to see what else I would like to do and begin to do that.

Daydream

Yes, this is a great way to raise your vibrations. Just going off into another world and imagining things to do, things to try, places to go, is sheer fun. As adults we should do that more. It's amazing the new stuff we can dream up when we day dream. And talking about dreams, if you keep a dream journal where you record the dreams you have at night and their meanings, interpretations and applications; these always inspire me and uplift me.

Now add some ways that you can use to change the way you feel and keep your vibrations high.

Action Step 6

1. Write down 20 things you are grateful for

2. Then do a meditation or prayer where you embrace the feelings of gratitude and you articulate your thanks to God for all His goodness.

3. Be intentional. Be focused and be completely in the moment.

PERSONAL NOTES

PERSONAL NOTES

Chapter 7 – Strategies for Wealth and Increase

You persuade people with passion, so you've got to have a product or service that you are passionate about. **Anita Roddick**

So here is where we take it beyond the ethereal and sit down to come up with practical ways to increase our income and our wealth.

The most important thing to remember here is that thinking is the highest paid form of work. This is because everything you do will originate from that space.

The next most important thing is to consider your gifts and abilities. You were given those gifts and abilities for a reason. You can think of ways you can use your gifts and abilities to serve other people. We are all put on this earth to serve each other. No one is independent of anyone else. We all need something that someone else provides. You may be a great songwriter but you can't sing for toffee. Hence you need a good singer to bring those songs to life. This is my position. I have written many songs, but don't have the best singing voice. But hey, why let that get in the way when there are so many talented singers I could ask to sing my songs? You may be a great fashion designer but you are not built for the catwalk. So you need a fashion model. You may be a brilliant mathematician but you cannot cook to save your life, so you need a cook. You get my point.

All of our gifts are not given for our own personal enjoyment. Our gifts are given so we can use them to enrich the world. They are also the way we make an income.

How can you use your abilities in a way that can be monetized? Then think about the various forms of producing your gift that can all be monetized. Then think about how you can maximise the amount of people that you reach and serve with your gift. This is because the more people you can serve with your gift and thereby receive monetary compensation, the more you are able to earn.

So this sum is the value you bring to others and how much they are willing to pay you, which equals your compensation.

In order to increase those values think of ways to add excellence to what you do and how to make its presentation even more attractive. Make sure that even though you are operating in your gift you do not neglect the need for quality. This means that you practise, you rehearse, and you take care. You want to develop expertise at what you do. Become known as an expert.

What is the point of having ability or a gift that others can benefit from but you are keeping to yourself? Do you honestly feel that is why you have been given your gift, to keep it to yourself? Let me tell you, it is not.

It is to serve others gladly and joyfully. You will be even more glad and joyful when they pay you.

They will pay you when you present it with excellence and skill. So get even better at what you do. Become known for it. Do not be a well kept secret.

Next think about separating yourself from the competition. That means those who have similar gifts and talents to you that may also be offering it in the market place. Make sure you can differentiate yourself. Discover and develop your USP. This is not a business book so we will not go into that here, however this is something you should learn more about and put into practice. It is important to stand out in your field and to stand out for the right reasons.

Make sure you also think of ways to scale up, meaning, ask yourself how you can continue doing what you do but for more people. If you can do this, you will be operating at an optimal level.

Find ways where you can do what you already do but in different formats, so you can be paid twice or more for what is really the same information. For example you could write a book and be paid for that; and you could also turn that book into a course and sell that at a higher price. There is plenty of scope.

Have a look in the market place and see who is doing what you want to do. Then study the top 5 providers of this service. Once you have done so, study how you can do the same but even better.

If you are having difficulty identifying your gift, think of what you do really well, better than most people, yet with the least amount of effort.

Start there. Start to practise it. How much better can you get at doing it? How can you excel at it? Start paying it attention. Develop excellence around it and examine how you can monetize it. Remember, your purpose is always tied to your gift. This will open many doors for you and many opportunities for wealth and success.

Everyone lives by selling something. **RL Stevenson**

Then remember to get good advice and counsel, take on a business coach, exercise due diligence and get started. As I said earlier, this is not a business book but I am here to help you raise your thinking around money and wealth to enable you to have a highly successful business should you decide to start one. You will never be successful as an entrepreneur or business person if your attitude to money is lacking or you do not understand the laws that govern success.

This book is not the entire deal. You will still need to learn to master business strategies and I would direct you towards a business coach for such.

Action Step 7

1. *Get your notebook out and come up with 5 things or more you can create that people would be happy to pay you for.*

2. *Consider what you are doing right now for free that you can charge for. It's time to value your gifts and abilities and stop giving them away. Put a value on it.*

PERSONAL NOTES

PERSONAL NOTES

Chapter 8 – How to Develop an Affinity for Money

"Don't tell me where your priorities are, show me where you spend your money and I'll tell you what they are." **James W Frick**

The first and foremost thing you must do to develop an affinity with wealth is to stop worrying.

This is one of the biggest things you must change.

Worrying means you are concerned that you do not have enough to take care of your needs.

Worrying means you are concerned you do not have sufficient to take care of your bills.

Worrying means you feel you cannot really have the things you want.

Worrying means you are not truly at peace.

Worrying is not in harmony with wealth or success.

Do you know any wealthy person who worries about not having enough money to take care of their affairs? You have to get out of the vibration of worry and anxiety. You must practice relaxation and peace. This is where I find such spiritual techniques including meditation and visualisation helps. Now you may say to me, "but I am no good at visualising and I am not sure I believe in meditation". Then let me ask you, what do you think worrying is? Worrying is imagining and visualising how things might go wrong, or how things might not work out the way you want.

Worry is fear at work in an overactive imagination. Do you know that the vast majority of things we worry about do not happen? That means you could save yourself all that mental energy and not worry in the first place.

You could use all that mental power to picture yourself having the things you need. You could visualise yourself doing well in your business. You could see yourself signing up new clients. You could imagine yourself signing a big contract. Think on these things instead.

Next begin to examine your environment. Does your environment look like one that is welcoming to wealth?

Do you need to make some changes?

Do you need to do some decluttering at all? Do you need to clear your space? Your outer world needs to reflect your inner world.

If your inner world is thinking thoughts of prosperity and wealth, your outer world needs to line up. This means you need to do as much as in your power to make ready for wealth and create an environment where good success is welcome.

Next, do your companions have a healthy attitude towards wealth? If they do not and you are spending significant time with them, this will only slow down the process. Work on your physical environment and work on your relational environment. Our friends have a great ability to impact the way we think and behave. Consider spending significant times only with people who are already where you want to be wealth wise or who are in agreement and alignment with all things of good success and wealth.

It doesn't mean you cut people off and you no longer talk to them. It means you do not spend so much time that they are influencing you back to your old ways of thinking and behaving.

Spend time with people that will have you up levelling your thinking and up levelling your expectations of life and up levelling your expectations of yourself.

Next go to places that wealthy people go to. Shop where they shop. It doesn't mean you buy things on your credit card and get into debt. It may be you buy something simple like a fragrance, or a silk scarf, or a body lotion. It should be something you can treat yourself to that gives you a foot into the door of wealthy living.

Train yourself to appreciate nice things. Train yourself to appreciate the arts and enjoy its beauty. Go to an art gallery and enjoy the skill and beauty of the painter and artist. Go to a top hotel and order afternoon tea. Begin developing new muscles.

Have you noticed that people who consider themselves poor do not have time to go to art galleries or do not treat themselves to quality fragrances? They tell themselves they don't have the money for such frivolities and they have better things to do.

Begin to change that thinking by telling yourself you do have time for the finer things in life and you are freely enjoying all things.

Study the types of people who do this kind of a thing regularly. What is their attitude? How are they different to you? How are they deporting themselves? How do they engage with other people? How confident are they? How relaxed are they? What can you take away from them and adopt for yourself.

How can you practice being wealthy before it actually unfolds fully in your life?

Action Step 8

Create today a 21 day action plan where you do something every day that puts you in harmony and affinity with wealth. That should include one daily action you can take that will bring you in proximity to those who are wealthy and the activities they do. This could be a light lunch at an upscale restaurant; it could be designer cologne; an evening at the theatre; or taking an exercise class at an expensive gym, etc.

PERSONAL NOTES

PERSONAL NOTES

Chapter 9 – A Giving Attitude

This is a small yet key chapter because here I want to talk about the spirit of giving.

Whilst we are focusing on acquiring wealth, it's important to note that having a willingness to give cheerfully is necessary. The great thing is you do not need to become rich before you give. You start where you are right now.

Being wealthy is not about accumulating as much as you can and keeping it all. It is about being in the wealth flow, engaging with the Law of Circulation.

Wealthy people are happy to give away money to charities or create their own charities. This is the healthy attitude towards wealth.

Be prepared to give away not just to family or friends because everyone does that. Find how to give to those beyond your circle and see how your wealth can really make a lasting difference.

Maybe you can volunteer at your local church; help out regularly in a charity shop; pay for someone's shopping; give to a food bank; give someone a gift you know they would love but they can't afford to buy, etc.

Perhaps you may want to provide educational scholarships for those who can't afford a good education; perhaps you may want to provide a music scholarship for those who are gifted in music but cannot afford to study; perhaps you may want to provides funds for a community centre that is in need of supplies; perhaps you may want to give money to provide shelter for the homeless; perhaps you may want to create a home for orphaned children. There are so many needs in the world and your ability to give would make a difference.

It is also good to give a portion away to the place where you receive your spiritual nourishment. Those who give us spiritual teaching and understanding often do so at a cost of working a regular day job, so giving to those who bless your life spiritually is a practical way of showing appreciation. God blesses those who tithe. It is His system of bringing wealth to you. A tithe is ten percent of your income. The best thing to do is to give it first, make it your priority, that way you don't say you don't have enough to time because it is all spent.

Action Step 9

If you do not already tithe, or give to charity, or make other charitable donations, begin now investigating how you can begin doing so. If you listen to teaching online many churches and charities have online giving.

PERSONAL NOTES

PERSONAL NOTES

Chapter 10 – The Laws that Govern Money

Getting rich is a science. **Wallace D Wattles**

One thing that I am learning is that becoming wealthy is an inside job.

The sacred text tells us that we are destroyed because of lack of knowledge.

In order to gain wealth and come out of poverty, scarcity and lack, it is necessary to become very aware of how wealth and money works. It is imperative to understand the laws of success.

This world works according to spiritual and scientific law. That is why it is orderly and runs perfectly without our help.

It is important for us to understand how these laws work and how we can cooperate with them in order to be successful in the world.

You would not join a company and never seek to find out the culture of the company, the company rules and policies, even the company mission.

It is necessary to understand this world that you are living in because in order to function successfully and at high levels you must understand the rules of the game. The more you understand the rules of the game the more likely you are to become a master of the game. Those who master the game can become leaders. Those leaders can train others to become leaders and so change the world.

You have a choice. You can follow the path that society has set out which is to get a 'good' education, work hard, and retire and then do what you enjoy in your final years. Or, you can find your own path, navigated by your spirit and intuition, work within your gift, learn how to monetize your gift and operate within the universal laws that govern success. Which do you choose?

We must understand that the laws have no favourite. They work for everyone. It doesn't matter whether you are young or old, black or white, male or female, you just have to work in accordance to the rules of success and you will succeed. It has to happen. It is the law.

So what laws do you need to be aware of? There are several and I will discuss a few of them in this chapter. You have already come across one in this book. Let us start with the <u>Law of Vibration</u>. This is actually the foundation law where everything else starts.

This Law states that we are not just our physical bodies but that we are spiritual beings and therefore we are vibrating energy all the time. The energy that we vibrate will connect us with other like energies. So if we are vibrating at any low frequency such as depression, sadness, anger, or fear of lack, we will attract the very same. This is because like attracts like. They say misery likes company, it's so true. We all know this. It works at every level. So for you to be successful and align yourself with wealth and success you cannot be thinking at the level of depression, fear, worry etc.

You must start putting out the energy of wealth and good success. See yourself as a wealthy individual. Create that picture and vision of yourself in your mind and heart. Regularly use affirmations which reinforce this.

Look at your friends and your general circle, are they a positive circle? You cannot spend quality time with people who love to complain and bemoan their situation and who always have a sob story. They will bring you down into their vortex. Pull yourself back up by finding those who are enjoying life and who are busy making things happen. People who are excited about life and are always looking ahead are the ones you want to connect and engage with. Make sure you no longer attract those who are negative and enjoy telling you how hard and how unfair life is. These conversations will not benefit you. Raise your vibrations and these people will no longer feel comfortable with you and you will no longer feel comfortable with them because you will be vibrating on different frequencies.

The Law of Attraction

This law is really based on the proverb 'as a man thinks so he is'. The law of attraction is that process whereby what we think about consistently we actually create.

The law of attraction works by whatever we send out in our words and in our thoughts and in our emotions we inherit the physical components.

This is why it is so important to govern our words and emotions. We cannot be out of control and let things spiral.

If life is becoming topsy turvy start looking at ways you can change your emotions, thoughts and your words because you will produce what you say. You also produce what you fear. Job in the bible declared that the very thing that he feared had come upon him. Fear is faith in reverse. It is expecting something bad to happen. It is opening your heart to the possibility of something you do not want. Do not focus on what you do not want. By regarding it and creating it in your mind you are giving it life. Cancel it and immediately replace with the opposite. Replace it with what you want to happen instead and focus and speak on that. Let the law of attraction work for you because it is always working, so make sure it works in your favour.

The Law of Thought

Yes there is a law of thought, it is very real and it works. Throughout this book I have stressed that thoughts are things.

There is a law that governs our thoughts and it's to our benefit to seek to understand it. Remember your thoughts affect your emotions and can affect your health. We know people who are depressed are thinking in a certain way. We know people who think bitter thoughts behave in a certain way. We know people who think happy thoughts behave in a certain way, in fact feeling happy even boosts our immune system whereas opposite thoughts help to bring our immunity down.

Every thought has its own energy, just like every word has its own energy. Think of how harsh, critical words affect the emotions when you are on the receiving end. Then think how loving and kind words affect the spirit when you hear them. Words and the thoughts they come from are important for us all to understand.

So find a way to condition your mind. The most effective way to do so is by meditation, relaxation and affirmation. Train your mind by the input of right thinking, by repetition of positivity and faith and using the power of affirmation to reinforce this.

Scientists tell us our heart has a mind of its own. So our hearts think too. In fact, that mind in our heart is stronger than the mind in our brain. So feeling is everything. Make sure your brain and your heart and are in agreement. So be careful what you take in and absorb.

The Law of Increase

Everything in this world that is alive is growing. If it is not growing it is dying. This is how the world works. We live in a world of constant expansion.

This law ensures that what we use grows and increases and what we neglect diminishes. The sacred text tells us that the person who has shall be given more. It also tells us that the time and attention we give to something will be measured back to us with increase.

This law of increase ensures that the more you attend to what you to, the greater the harvest. The more you are grateful and appreciate of what you have the more you will get to be grateful for.

This works by rewarding your efforts. So apply yourself to what you do. Make your light shine. Do not hide it underneath a bush but put it where it can be seen and can give light to many.

Use your resources to produce more. Use your gifts to produce more. Do not bury your gift. If you use your gift you will find yourself with more. This is the Law of Increase at work.

The Law of Forgiveness

This law is one we all need to be aware of because throughout our wealth journey we will have plenty of opportunity to be offended or hurt by someone. The worse thing we can do is to harbour feelings of hate, animosity and bitterness in our hearts. Carrying unforgiveness is like drinking poison and expecting it to hurt someone else. You are the one drinking the poison so it will hurt you. Holding on the resentment will just hurt you.

Often we feel justified in holding onto our feelings of rage and hate because we have been done wrong. But we must come to recognise that we do not forgive because they deserve it but we forgive because we need to be free emotionally and mentally. We cannot afford to carry so much negativity in our hearts and spirit.

Unforgiveness is a negative energy which invites further negativity into our lives. It holds us back and it ensures that our perceptions and outlook is off key. Our vision is obscured and our heart is not clear.

Make the decision to forgive, which is to release that person in your mind and heart and let it go. You deserve to have peace and serenity again live in your heart and mind. Why carry the pain of bitterness and hurt when you can be free?

The Law of Success

It is necessary to understand that God intended everyone to succeed. He did not plan for anyone to come into this world to fail. It's His will that you should enjoy the fullness of the world He created. He created the entire world for mankind. You have God given faculties within you that if developed and maximised will bring increasing success.

To do that you must know what these faculties are. You already know you have your five senses but you have much more than that. You cannot live from the five physical senses alone. You must let the spiritual part of you direct the physical.

Here are your spiritual faculties:-

Perception; that is the way you look at life.

Your Will; you have your free moral will whereby you make choices, whereby you concentrate and take decisions.

Reason; you have your sense of reason which allows you to apply rationale and logic. Memory; you have your memory which allows you acquire, store and recall information. Imagination; you also have your imagination which allows you to create experiences and create an entire world within your mind. It is a creative power that enables you to invent something that does not yet exist.

These faculties give you the optimal potential to do amazing things. God wants you to increase, to succeed, and to take dominion in all things.

You must study these laws and apply them. These laws work. They have no other choice. They are God ordained and set.

If you want to succeed and you want to discover the wealth you can enjoy, you must delve into the power of cooperating with these laws. They always work because nature is perfect.

Action Step 10

Learn all the above laws in detail. Make it your priority to understand them thoroughly. Become very familiar about them all.

PERSONAL NOTES

PERSONAL NOTES

Chapter 11 - Money, Wealth and You

In this final chapter I want to really connect you to a new version of yourself. I want you to forget the old you that has been struggling so far. I don't care how much you have tried and it has not worked. I don't care how life has tested and tried you so far. I want you to know that life can change for you now as soon as you decide you want to change.

This book does not have to be like the ones you have read in the past. That is to say, I do not want you read it and be inspired and then set it down and carry on with life as you have done in the past. What you have done so far has brought you to where you are today.

To get different results you must do something different.

The difference with this book is that you will not just read it but you will make the quality decision to do things differently from now on.

You will decide that wealth is your portion. You will decide wealth is a strong possibility for you. You will decide that wealth is totally appropriate for someone like you. You will decide that God is glorified through your success and not through your failure. You will decide from today to let you light shine so that men will see it and glorify your creator.

You will decide that the abundant life is for you. You will decide that good things are for you. You will decide that the good life is for you. You will decide that you are going onwards and upwards in life. You will decide that you will, if need be, become the first person in your family to be wealthy. You will decide that you will create a pathway for generational wealth for your household.

You will decide that you will rise up and demand more from life.

You will decide that you will no longer just receive what is given but you will rise up take what you want.

You will decide that you are a leader and not a follower. You will decide that now is the time for you and your generation to be wealthy. You will decide that this is the moment for things to change for your good. You will decide that life is going to work in your favour.

You will decide to start to feel wealthy knowing that the feeling of wealth will attract wealth to you.

You will decide that now is the time for you to win and to win big. You will decide that whatever you do produces good fruit and good success.

You will decide that you will prosper, be healthy and continue to increase in every way.

You will decide that you will give and you will receive bountifully.

You will decide that you will enjoy the riches around you and that money is always circulating around you.

You have accepted that wealth is a state of mind just as poverty is a state of mind. You will decide to develop a wealthy state of mind.

Note well. Please give yourself time. It will not change in 24 hours. In order to redress and reverse years of wrong conditioning you must be prepared to put in the time to recondition your mind. Take time to renew your mind. This is not a book about instant riches. Do not try this for a week or a month and say it doesn't work, if you don't get wealthy in a month. Commit three to six months minimum to putting this to work. I guarantee it will begin making itself seen and heard within that time. The key is consistency and application. This is where many fail. Remember, everything is a process. Nature is a process. You plant the seed today and in its season it grows. Please give this process due time and you will reap if you faint not.

These laws do not fail.

Action Step 11

Find people that you resonate with and connect with them. Listen to their social media. Listen to their podcasts or their songs or their YouTube. Begin to imbibe from them.

Just pick one or two people and follow their broadcasts etc regularly until your energy is on the same level as them.

Possible people may be

Patrice Washington

Dennis Kimbro

Joseph McClendon

Sandy Gallagher

Dr George Fraser

Melanie Benson

Tiphani Montgomery

Talane Meidaner

PERSONAL NOTES

PERSONAL NOTES

Chapter 12 - Affirmations and Decrees for Wealth

Life and death are in the power of the tongue and those who love it will eat its fruit. Proverbs 18.21

This chapter is simply a list of affirmations that can be used to build a wealth consciousness. Affirmations are a way of using the Law of Repetition. Whatever you want to create in your life, the process of repeatedly focusing upon it will create exponential results.

As you give wealth your attention, you will vibrate in harmony with it. This is how you become aligned to what you seek

Affirmations for wealth will program your subconscious mind for wealth.

1. God's plan for me is good success, to give me a future and a hope.
2. All things are possible to those who believe and I believe.
3. Wealth and success are mine and I have wealthy and successful ideas.
4. God moves through me to do his will and his good pleasure.
5. As a man thinks so he is. I think I am wealthy therefore I become wealthy every day.
6. I live in line with my beliefs and values.
7. I am happy for the success and wealth of others and there is more than enough for everyone including me.
8. I decree wealth and it is established for me.

9. I make alive the truths of God by feeling them in my heart. I am truly rich and blessed because I know God.

10. I move from poverty to abundance thinking

11. Money comes expectedly and unexpectedly

12. Wealth creates positive impact in my life

13. I am at peace with handling a lot of money

14. My finances improve beyond my dreams

15. Wealth constantly flows into my life

16. I release all negativity around money.

17. I release all negativity around wealth

18. I welcome new avenues of income.

19. Opportunities for wealth come to me daily.

20. I am aligned with abundance.

21. I am aligned with wealth.

22. God blesses me daily.

23. My cup is full and running over with grace.

24. I am surrounded with favour like a shield.

25. I have a good relationship with wealth.

26. My actions create constant prosperity.

27. God takes delight in my prosperity.

28. Financial freedom and peace of mind are mine.

29. I am at peace because God is my supply.

30. I believe God has given me all I need to succeed.

31. Financial miracles happen for me all the time.

32. My thoughts are creative and I think of wealth.

33. God has given me all things richly to enjoy.

34. My words and meditation are pleasing to God

35. Life is a gift to me. I am here to express life.

36. I am here to express the God in me through my God given gifts.

37. My thought image is wealth and good success.

38. Where focus goes energy flows. I focus on wealth and good success.

39. I choose life so that I may live.

40. Creating wealth is second nature to me.

41. Every day is a wealthy day.

42. I attract clients who are excited to work with me.

43. Wealth is a God idea.

44. Being wealthy is my nature.

45. God has made me wealthy so I can help humanity.

46. Every day my wealth is increasing in accordance with the law of increase.

47. The God of heaven prospers me.

48. I am the head and not the tail, the above and not the beneath.

49. The Lord God is my Shepherd and I shall not want.

50. Every need is met and supplied.

51. My desires are met because God grants the desires of my heart.

52. I dwell on the idea of increasing good so I can do more in life.

53. Good ideas for witty inventions come to me all the time.

54. I wish increase and success for others.

55. There is no limit to what I am capable of earning.

56. Money comes to me in all ways from sources known and unknown.

57. I give and it's given to me pressed down, shaken together and running over.

58. Money loves to be around me and I am an excellent host to wealth.

59. I am a wise money manager and all my monies increase.

60. I choose to help others unselfishly.

61. I live in a world of constant supply.

62. Nature is lavish and bountiful and there is always more than enough.

63. I love beautiful things and I surround myself with such.

64. God created the world and said it was good. My world is good and I have every good thing.

65. Every day I am inspired by God.

66. Every day I am blessed with peace and serenity

67. Every day grace is multiplied to me and always flowing.

68. Peace of mind is mine.

69. I go out with joy and I am led by peace

70. I know that God is blessing me in all ways.

71. I am daily experiencing the blessings of the fruit of the spirit.

72. I am one with God who is the source of life.

73. In God I live and move and have my being.

74. All that God has is mine and I rejoice that this is so.

75. I walk with a healthy and wealthy state of mind.

76. I keep thinking of God's wealth which is all around me.

77. I keep my attention on whatsoever things are lovely and of good report.

78. I get acquainted with the rich life inside me by confessing its reality.

79. I walk in faith because faith has works.

80. The fullness of God is made manifest in all aspects of my life.

81. I radiate abundance to others.

82. Wealth is in the air I breathe.

83. My life blossoms like the rose.

84. I walk in the consciousness of God's love

85. I am deeply grateful for the wealth that comes into my life.

86. I am grateful every day for all my blessings.

87. I am blessed to be a blessing to others.

88. The world is a wonderful place to be and I am blessed to be here. I will make the most of my time here in every way I can.

89. I start every day by giving thanks with a grateful heart.

90. I say that I am strong and I say that I am rich.
    Wealth comes to me honestly and with integrity.

91. I place no limits on what I can do because I can do all things through God.

92. The sky is not a limit but a beautiful view.

93. I stir up daily the gift of God that is in me.

94. I am a legitimate child of God and deserve good things. Everything in my father's house is mine. I can enjoy them at any time.

95. I inhale the peace of God and exhale his love.

96. Wealth and riches are in my house.

97. Today is a great day to be wealthy.

98. Wealth and prosperity flow through every area of my life.

99. This one thing I do, forgetting the past, I press towards the mark of God's high call

100. I am blessed and highly favoured.

PERSONAL NOTES

PERSONAL NOTES

Frequently Asked Questions about Wealth

Q1. Is it enough to just affirm and visualise wealth in order to be wealthy.

If we could just think about it that would be great however faith without works is dead. God definitely wants you do well but he doesn't bless slothfulness or laziness. So whatever you are visualising and affirming, it is important that your actions are in line with it too. With that being the case, take all and every inspired action that will take you into the direction of your dreams and desires.

Q2. I find it hard to maintain my positivity when it doesn't happen right away.

This is the where so many people fall down. They start off doing well, with plenty of faith, making great affirmations and describing their dreams and goals. Then when it doesn't happen within a week or a month they stop and think it is not working for them. What must be understood is that everything in nature is a process. Things do not happen at the snap of a finger. What you must do is put things in place and trust the process. That is where you stand on your faith, having done everything, keep standing, and do not retreat.

It is important to remember to keep the words that we say in line with our prayers, affirmations and declarations. We cannot pray one thing when we are feeling good, spiritual and strong and then go out and indulge in negative and idle conversation. We must be congruent in all our ways. Examine what you say. Are you always saying "there's never enough", "I never succeed"? If so, you must change your confession.

Q3. How important is it to give when you are already having a tough time.

Giving matters because you need to get into the flow of circulation. Money needs to circulate. You cannot hold on to it and think you will enjoy abundance and enjoy increase. Give and it will be given unto you. That is a spiritual law. Give according to your means. Do not go crazy. If money is severely limit then give away your time, because time is money. Perhaps give away a skill for free and give that way. Start somewhere. You will never lose if you become a giver, because God will not be a debtor to anyone and He always repays.

Q4. How can I become comfortable with having a lot of money? I was raised to just ask for what I need.

Be aware that money is here to serve you. The more money you have the more you are able to do and accomplish. Of course if you were raised very frugal then you have learned to set your expectations low so it will take a minute to recondition your mind to abundance. This is where affirmations come in. Reading the bible and covering all the scriptures on prosperity will help. The bible is full of accounts of people who were extremely rich. Also become comfortable with giving money away and enjoy being a blessing to others.

Q5. I was raised believing the love of money is the root of all evil. I don't want to focus on the wrong thing.

The interesting thing here is that many people with little money think about money all the time. They think about how they are going to get enough of it to pay their bills. They think about it when they worry how they are going to put food on the table. They think about it when they ruminate on how they are going to pay their child's school fees. People with wealth rarely worry about such things. They are more concerned with enjoying the fruit of their labour which the bible says is their right or they are concerned with how they can use their wealth to help others on the planet. You choose which one of these is the better place to put your focus. And remember, God has no problem with money at all. In fact, money is a God idea. Wealth is a God idea. Poverty and insufficiency are not from God and are not things you should get used to accepting in your life.

Q.6 Why did Jesus ask the rich ruler to give away his money in order to follow him? Doesn't this mean we cannot be rich and spiritual?

First of all be aware that Jesus was not broke or poverty stricken. In fact he had a treasurer; you do not need a treasurer if you have no money. When they crucified him they cast lots for his robe because it was very expensive. The example we have here is someone not having their priorities straight. You cannot put money ahead of God. Money is here to serve you. Money is not here for you to serve it. This is why it is important to be a giver and not a hoarder. God does not promote poverty so be aware this is all about priorities. Simply put God first in your life because He is your source and the fount of every blessing you receive.

Final Note from Dr Patricia

I have so loved writing this book. It is a book that I am absolutely passionate about. It is one of my mandates. It is something I am commissioned to share and release to as many as possible.

I want you to no longer be happy with just getting by. I want you to recognise that you do not have to be satisfied with your lot if your lot is limited and sparse. Where did all that thinking come from? Where did we learn to accept little and think it was a virtue to settle with it and await happiness in a world was to come? Where did we learn to accept jam tomorrow but only tomorrow never comes?

I want to really impress the idea that you can develop spiritual, mental and emotional muscles that will pull you up from where you are and pull you into the greater arena of good success and always having more than enough in every situation. I want you to go from being in need of a financial breakthrough or being in need of a financial turn around to being the source of someone else's turnaround.

I want you to recognise that God is not far away, but that He is with you at all times and will help you and guide you in all your endeavours. The scriptures tell us to acknowledge Him in all our ways and He will direct our paths. He does not direct us into poverty and scarcity.

Start to pray big prayers. You cannot pray too big for God. You cannot ever test God. God is too big, too incredible, too amazing and too awesome for you to send up these small and measly prayers. It's time for you now to level up.

Allow this book to be a kick starter to your prosperity. Allow it to encourage you to change your behaviours and your surroundings if they are negative. Work on building your inner man and your inner resources so that you are bigger than your environment so that it no longer affects you until you can vacate it totally. Your life will change and become unrecognizable.

I would be so delighted to hear from you about how this book has helped you and how you are doing things differently.

If you are interested in attending a Highly Fabulous Wealth Workshop or Wealth Empowerment Workshop then please email me for upcoming dates at Wealth@highlyfabulouswomen.com

Also if you would love for me to come to your organisation, ministry, or women's conference to share more in depth on this please write to me at drpatriciabenjamin@highlyfabulouswomen.com

In the meantime visit me at www.highlyfabulouswomen.com and be inspired and motivated to live highly fabulously.

Follow Dr Patricia on social media at Instagram ask-patricia

Twitter @IamAskPatricia

www.ingramcontent.com/pod-product-compliance
Lightning Source LLC
Chambersburg PA
CBHW022023170526
45157CB00003B/1326